MARSH MADNESS

A lighthearted look at the wacky world of waterfowling

Bruce Cochran

WILLOW CREEK PRESS

For the Lone Oak Duck Club

Published by Willow Creek Press
P.O. Box 147, Minocqua, Wisconsin 54548
www.willowcreekpress.com

Printed in Canada

Preseason Exercises
FOR **YOU** AND **YOUR DOG**

Get your fingers toughened up for duck plucking by pulling handfuls of hair out of your chest.

Make sure there's no gas in your chain saw, then pull the cord repeatedly to get your arm (and your vocabulary) in shape for dealing with that balky outboard motor.

Wet your dog down thoroughly, then step into his kennel with him. This will allow him to practice shaking off near you, thoroughly soaking YOU in the process.

Sear your oral membranes in preparation for duck blind coffee by gargling with drain cleaner once a day.

A rigid program of stretching exercises will enable old Buster to lick himself in places he could never reach before.

Toughen up your feet for those uncomfortable hours in leaky hip boots by standing in a tub of ice water for an hour each day.

Hone your shooting eye by mounting an imaginary
shotgun and "shooting" at pigeons in the park.
Make sure there are no policemen or psychiatrists around.

New gear FOR A NEW SEASON

Not enough room in your blind bag for all your essential gear? Free up some interior space with the DONUT LANYARD.
Holds 24 - 36 glazed donuts*.
Available in Mossy Oak Break-Up or Shadow Grass.

*Youth model holds 48.

Going after those urban honkers on the golf course?
You need 18th GREEN, the new
laydown blind in GOLF COURSE CAMO.
Comes with 6 ft. pin and red "18" flag.

Why stop with dressing your retriever in a neoprene vest? Old Buster will be the snazziest dude in the marsh with his new NEOPRENE VEST, BOW TIE, and BOOTIES.

Older goose hunters who have trouble sitting up
quickly to shoot will welcome
EJECTO-BLIND,
the first laydown blind equipped with an ejection seat.
Available in Shadow Grass and Corn Stubble.

Little-Known

If all the spinning wing decoys in the country were harnessed to produce electricity they would provide enough power to fill the needs of seven states for the entire duck season.

Duck hunters often hear mallards chuckling while flying overhead. Contrary to popular opinion this is not a "feeding chuckle." The ducks are actually laughing at us.

Banded gadwall hens have been known
to remove their leg bands because they
felt the bands made them look fat.

Beginning next season, hunters who refer
to widgeons as "baldpates" will be required
to take ten hours of sensitivity training.

When no one is looking, pintail drakes often remove one of their long tail feathers and use it for a tooth pick.

In the fall of '03, while attempting to migrate, a mallard drake left South Dakota and wound up on Iwo Jima. Being male, he never stopped to ask directions.

During the '01 season, a white duck, wearing a sailor hat and shirt (but no pants), was bagged by a Minnesota hunter. The event was kept quiet for fear of reprisals from a large entertainment corporation.

Duck hunters who miss opening day because of family obligations have been known to curl up in the fetal position and suck their thumbs for weeks at a time.

A coot once migrated from Alberta to Texas without ever getting more than five feet off the ground.

TRAINING YOUR RETRIEVER PUP

When Pup is very young
you should teach him to sit.

Pup should be housebroken
as soon as possible.

Pup should be retrieving dummies
by the time he's six months old.

Don't become discouraged when
Pup goes through his chewing phase.

Lots of playtime will help strengthen
the bonds between pup and owner.

Pup's introduction to birds will be
an exciting time in his young life.

Pup's introduction to water should be as pleasant as possible.

Pup can be taught to respond to the whistle by rewarding him with a treat.

TWEEEET

Pup's first ride in the car should
be a memorable experience.

Pup's introduction to the gun
should be handled with extreme care.

Don't be disturbed when Pup retrieves household objects and brings them to you.

Pup should become socialized by being around other people as much as possible.

By the time Pup is a year old he should be ready to hunt... or not.

Words of

Waterfowling Wisdom

From

Gadwall Gallagher, noted wing shot and editor of "Take 'Em!" magazine.

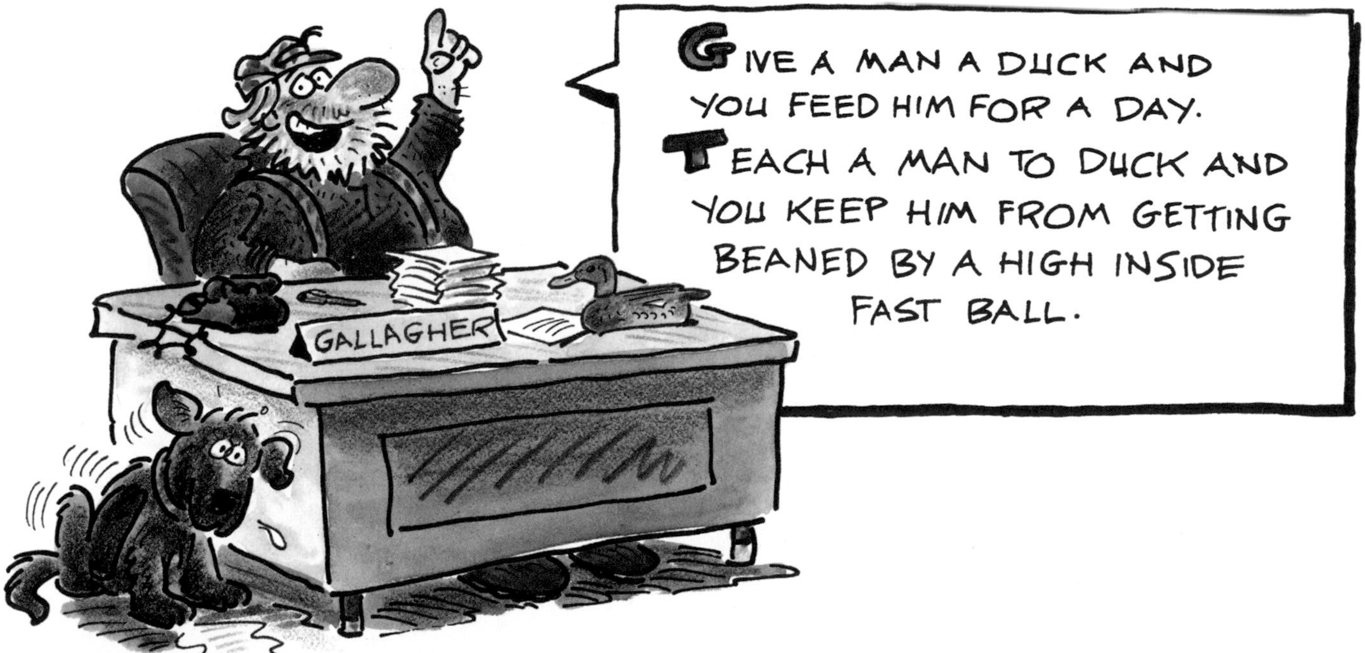
Give a man a duck and you feed him for a day. Teach a man to duck and you keep him from getting beaned by a high inside fast ball.
GALLAGHER

MANY Country & Western STARS ARE Duck Hunters. SOME EVEN INCORPORATE HUNTING THEMES INTO THEIR MUSIC.

HERE'S A LITTLE SONG I WROTE MYSELF. I CALL IT "YOU'RE THE MUSKRAT WHO TOOK A DUMP IN THE DUCK BLIND OF MY HEART."

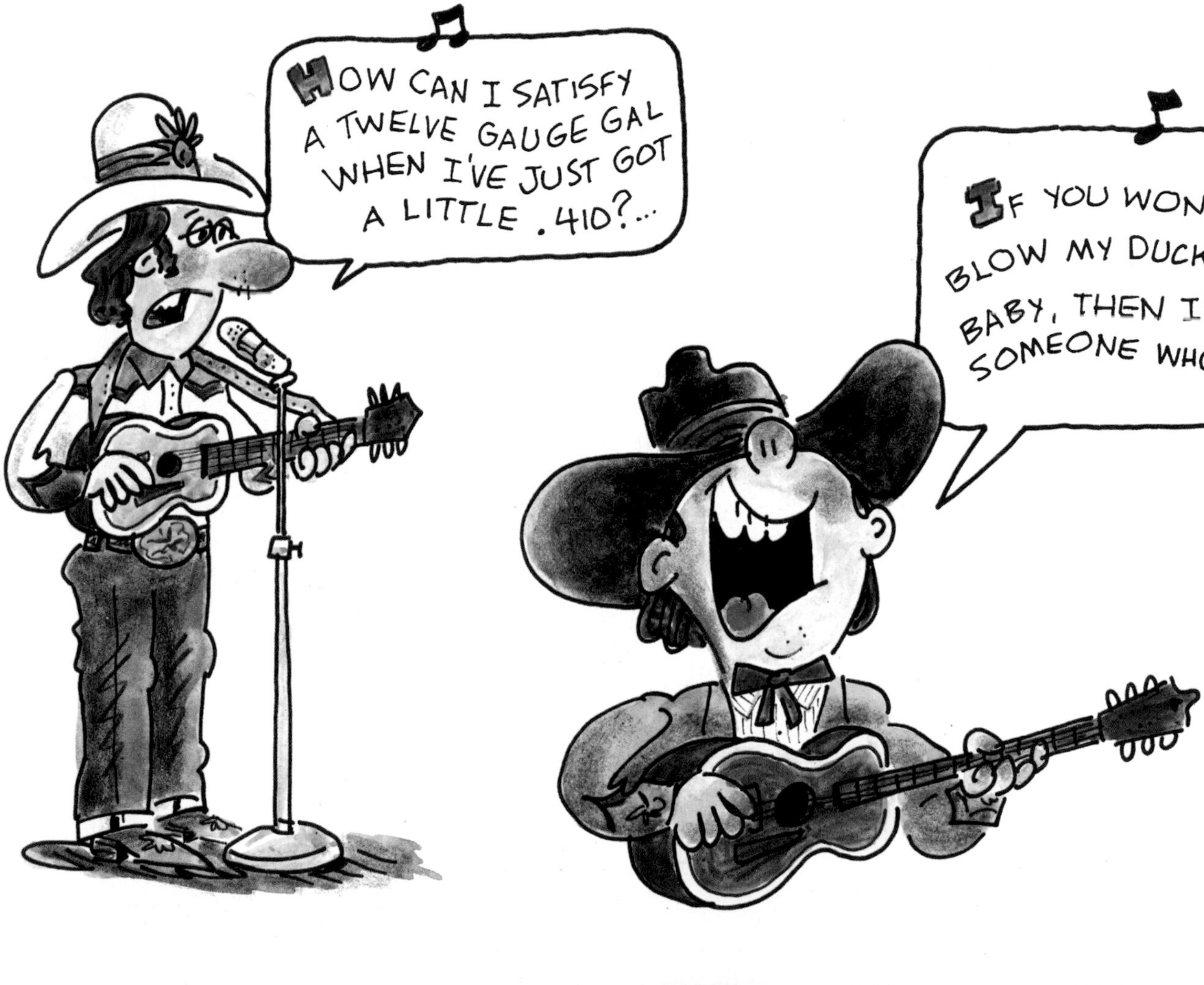
HOW CAN I SATISFY A TWELVE GAUGE GAL WHEN I'VE JUST GOT A LITTLE .410?...
IF YOU WON'T BLOW MY DUCK CALL, BABY, THEN I'LL FIND SOMEONE WHO WILL...

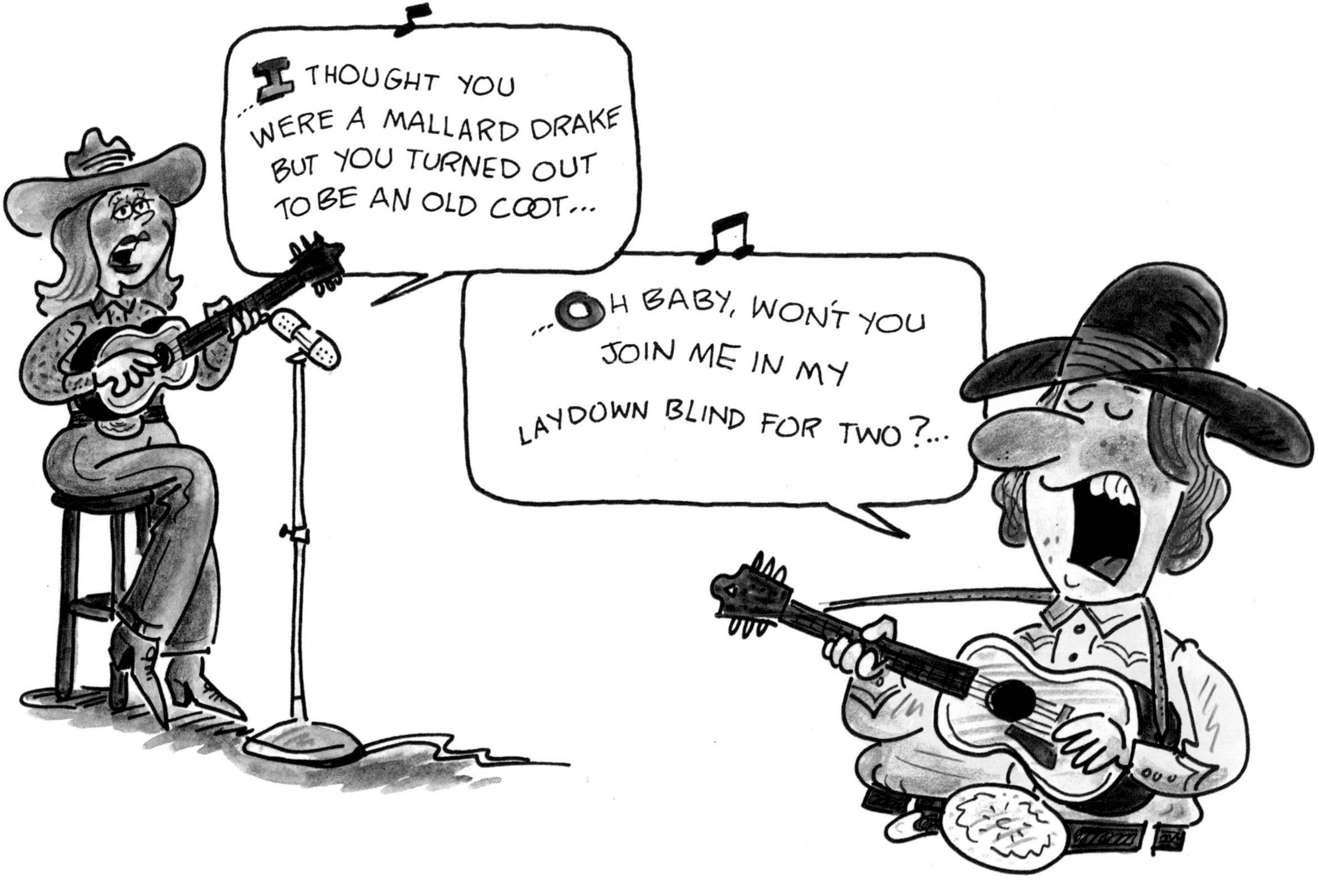
...I THOUGHT YOU WERE A MALLARD DRAKE BUT YOU TURNED OUT TO BE AN OLD COOT...
...OH BABY, WON'T YOU JOIN ME IN MY LAYDOWN BLIND FOR TWO?...

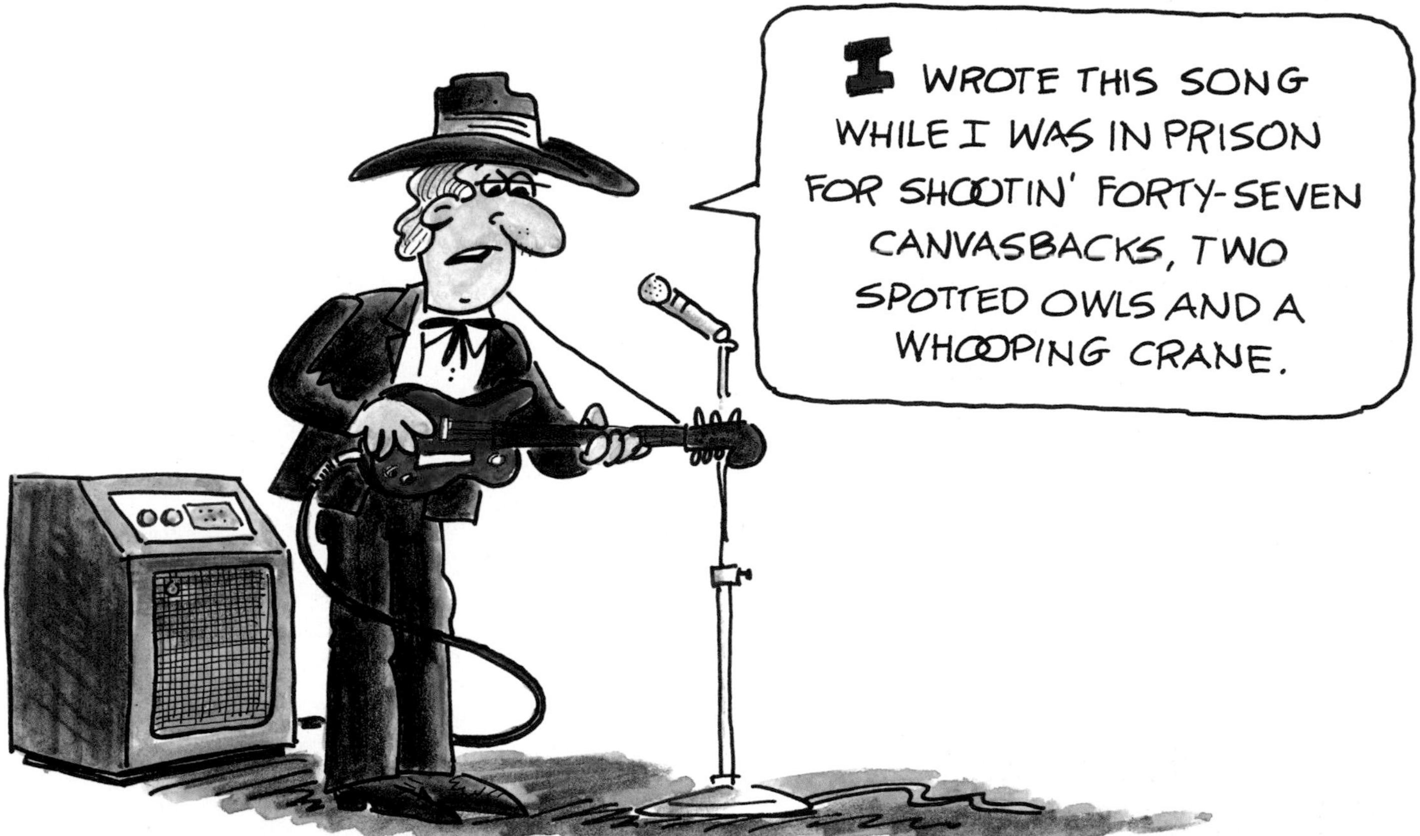
I WROTE THIS SONG WHILE I WAS IN PRISON FOR SHOOTIN' FORTY-SEVEN CANVASBACKS, TWO SPOTTED OWLS AND A WHOOPING CRANE.

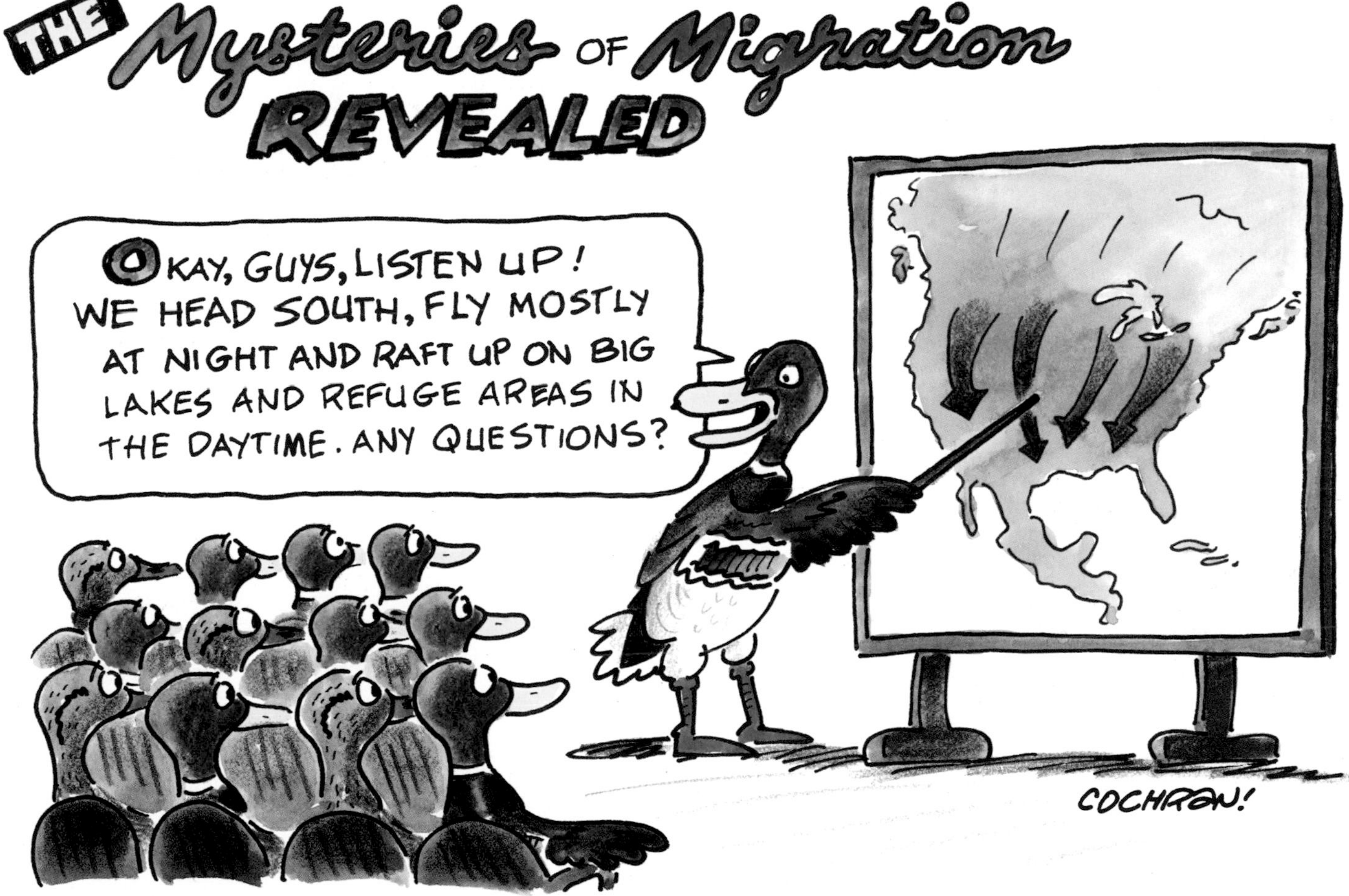
THE Mysteries OF Migration REVEALED
OKAY, GUYS, LISTEN UP! WE HEAD SOUTH, FLY MOSTLY AT NIGHT AND RAFT UP ON BIG LAKES AND REFUGE AREAS IN THE DAYTIME. ANY QUESTIONS?
COCHRAN!

25 THINGS YOU'LL NEVER HEAR A DUCK HUNTER SAY—

1. More decoys? Not me.
   I've got enough already.

2. This coffee is TOO hot!

3. I'm sleeping in this morning.
   That north wind is too cold for me.

4. Better walk from here.
   That mud looks bad.

5. Who wants this leg band.
I never keep 'em.

6. You see one greenhead dropping
in over the decoys... (yawn)...
you've seen them all.

7. This sunrise doesn't
do a thing for me.

8. I'll trade you my woody
drake for your shoveler hen.

9. You're right, Bob. Your dog
IS better than mine.

10. A new camo pattern?
Who needs it?

11. Why would I want another
waterfowl print on my wall?

12. I've never paid more than
$20 for a duck call in my life.

13. I HATE Gortex!

14. So you hear honkers flying over. Big deal.

15. I'm not going to bid on any of these auction items. I don't NEED anything.

16. What this sport needs is more regulations.

17. I need a smaller blind bag.

18. I'm not spending one more dollar on duck hunting stuff!

19. Hunting is okay, but I'd rather be playing bridge with my wife and her friends.

20. Go ahead, Harry, Step out of the blind. Ducks NEVER come in when we don't expect it.

21. I've got so much yogurt and tofu in my blind bag, there's no room for HoHos and Ding Dongs.

23. Who needs a retriever? They're more trouble than they're worth.

22. I'll stay in the blind for an hour. Then I'm leaving to go watch daytime television.

24. Let ME carry the decoys, Fred.

25. Sorry I'm going to miss duck season, fellas, my wife and I have a two month vacation in Romania planned.

There are many **SUBSPECIES** of **CANADA GEESE.** Some of the lesser known are...

THE LOPEZ GOOSE

SCHWARZENEGGER'S GOOSE

THE ELVIS GOOSE

THE CHERNOBLE GOOSE

BUBBA'S GOOSE

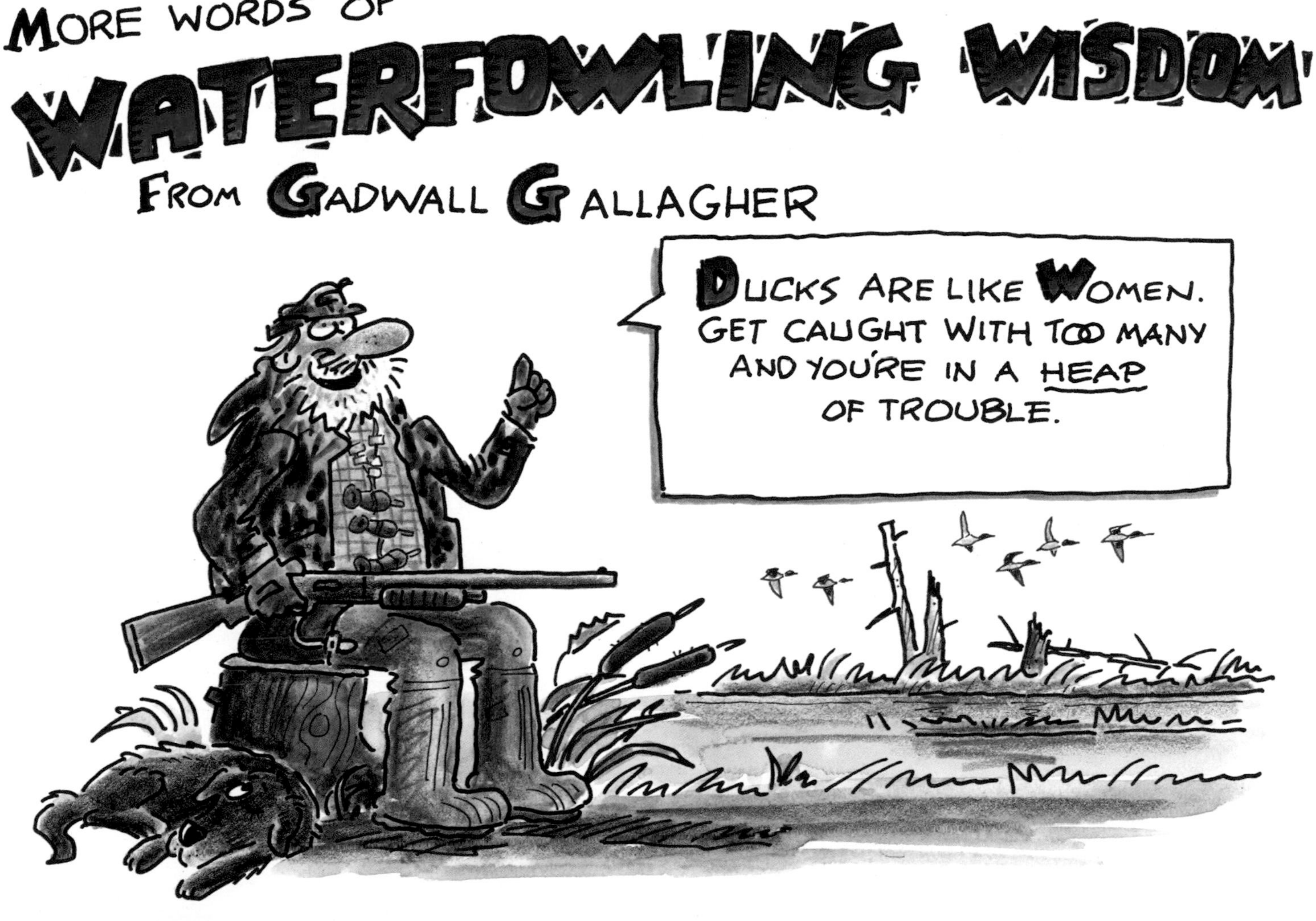
MORE WORDS OF
WATERFOWLING WISDOM
FROM GADWALL GALLAGHER
DUCKS ARE LIKE WOMEN. GET CAUGHT WITH TOO MANY AND YOU'RE IN A HEAP OF TROUBLE.

HAIKUS FOR THE DUCK HUNTER

Haikus are three line, seventeen syllable Japanese poems. Five syllables in the first line, seven in the second, and five more in the third. On slow days you can while away those hours in the duck blind by composing your own duck hunting haikus.

It had a green head when I shot it. Don't know how it got so damn brown.

Maggie. Babe. Shadow. Splash. Ebony. Tar. Sailor. What's your black Lab's name?

My leg is getting cold and wet. I should have patched these damn chest waders.

Muddy dog. Wet socks. Smelly camo coat. Big fire. Man! That's happiness.

Squawk! Bleep! Screech! Ka-Honk! Damn duck call! Oh wait! I am blowing the wrong end.

Her beauty dwarfs that of those around her. My girl friend? No. My black Lab.

What's black and lays on the couch eleven months of the year? Yep. My Lab.

Zip! Zoom! What the hell was that?? A jet? No, just a little flock of teal.

Bang! Bang! Bang! Three ducks fall. The guys on TV just don't miss. Unlike me.

Stomp! Crash! Splash! Shiver!
Damn I hate ice! Unless of
course it's in a drink.

Hey! Get your black nose
out of my blind bag. That was
MY sandwich! Too late...

Patterned my shotgun.
There is a big duck-shaped hole
right in the middle.

Take a boy hunting.
But if he outshoots you, leave
him at home next time.

New camo pattern,
makes you look like a blob of
mud. Sure. I'll buy one.

Season opener.
Tomorrow. Don't oversleep.
Get real! Who can sleep?!

Whistling through the trees.
I never got my gun up.
Now they're gone. Wood ducks.

Dead bird. Fetch it up.
No no! Not that! That's a dead
muskrat, you dumb butt.

So alert. Whining.
Her brown eyes pleading with me.
SHOOT SOMETHING FOR ME!

BEGINNING NEXT SEASON THE
FISH & WILDLIFE SERVICE
WILL IMPLEMENT A **NEW PLAN** FOR
MONITORING WATERFOWL HUNTERS....

PLEASE COOPERATE BY ALWAYS WEARING YOUR
ELECTRONIC LEG BAND WHILE HUNTING.

You know you're a REAL Duck Hunter when...

You're holding up a limit of greenheads in your driver's license photo.

Your retriever comes from a better family than you do.

You're registered for wedding gifts at Cabela's and Gander Mountain.

You paid more for a duck call than for your wife's engagement ring.

Your license plate is H2OFOWL, PINTAIL, or BLUBILL.

You take all your vacation days in duck season.

Your job has nothing to do with waterfowl but your business card has a duck on it.

All the new clothes you've bought
for the last ten years are camo.

You name your first child Drake...
even if she's a girl.

You send Christmas cards with hunting scenes on them to your non-hunting friends (if you have any).

You walk through mud better than you do on a sidewalk.

You own four sets of cocktail glasses, ten ties, fourteen shirts, three lamp shades, a wastebasket, two calendars, twenty paintings, eight coffee cups, seventeen baseball caps, five belt buckles, two decks of playing cards, seven pocket knives, a throw rug, and two wrist watches with ducks, geese, or dogs on them.

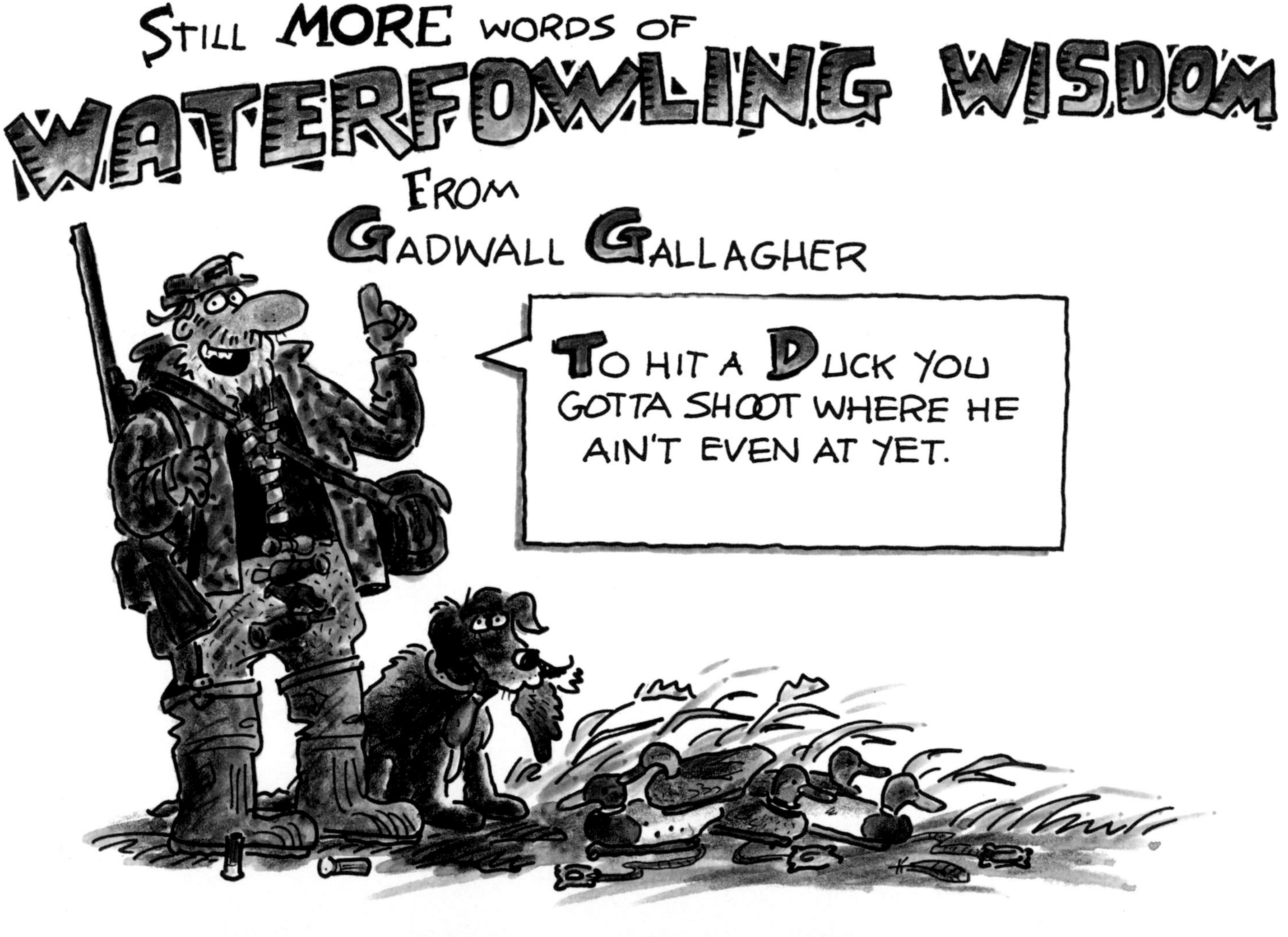
STILL MORE WORDS OF
WATERFOWLING WISDOM
FROM
GADWALL GALLAGHER
TO HIT A DUCK YOU GOTTA SHOOT WHERE HE AIN'T EVEN AT YET.

With his philandering ways it's only a matter of time until a mallard drake, looking for a little excitement, breeds with a chicken. Perhaps a tawny Rhode Island Red or a sultry Leghorn will strike his fancy. And when that happens the waterfowling world will be blessed with a new game bird...

THE CHUCK

Part chicken, part duck, this gaudy love child will revolutionize the world of duck hunting. And, as in most revolutions, there will be pluses and minuses.

PLUSES	MINUSES
Bigger drumsticks	Less challenging target
Protected as a game bird so cannot be sold at KFC	Looks funny when mounted on wall
Easier to hit	Your retriever will give you a funny look when sent to fetch one
More meat on wings	
Less nest predation (just lock the hen house door)	Non-webbed feet make it a poor swimmer*

*Some chucks could have one webbed foot and one non-webbed foot, in which case they would swim in a circle.

THIS HAPPENED TO ME!

HARROWING TALES OF NARROW ESCAPES IN THE DANGEROUS WORLD OF DUCK HUNTING!

It was barely 8 AM when I realized my retriever had eaten all my junk food while I was dozing. Luckily I had eaten Mexican food the night before so I survived the rest of the day by licking guacamole and salsa off my mustache.

Against my vet's advice, I took my female Lab hunting while she was in heat. During the morning we were attacked by forty-seven coyotes, two timber wolves, a feral cocker spaniel, and a confused raccoon.

While cleaning a limit of greenheads, my wife caught me using her sewing scissors for game shears, snatched them from my hands, and attempted to perform an impromptu medical procedure on me.

After playing poker 'til 2 AM the night before, I fell asleep in my layout boat and missed the morning flight, lunch, dinner, and the rest of the season.

While I was using a cow silhouette to sneak up on
a feeding flock of snow geese, a farmer tried to milk me.

Offended by my decals and bumper stickers, an anti-hunter attacked me in a parking lot, raising a large knot on my head and destroying my Nash Buckingham bobble head doll.

While relieving myself behind the blind a large snake crawled into my waders. Unaware of the snake, I pulled up my waders and returned to the blind. When my partner saw the snake slither out of the top of my waders he suffered a heart attack and I had to drive him to the hospital after the morning flight was over.

THE Duck Blind FOOD PYRAMID

SNUFF
LITTLE DEBBIES
HOHOS
CHEWING TOBACCO
DING DONGS
CIGARS
DONUTS
COFFEE
CINNAMON ROLLS

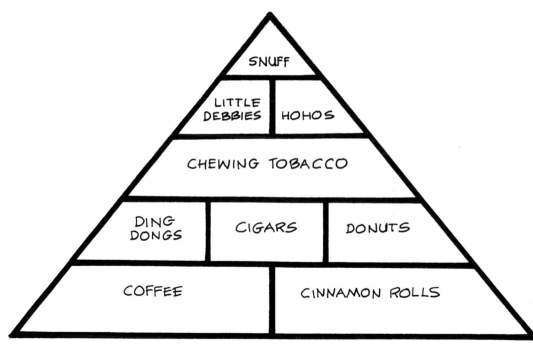

You've read **Water Dog**, **Gun Dog**, **Family Dog**, but what about **YOUR DOG?**...

LEG DOG
You can't take him ANYWHERE.

COUCH DOG

Any time she's not hunting you'll find her
faithfully manning her position.

Never leave anything lying on the ground when PEE DOG is around.

Want a nice lawn with shrubs and flowers? Forget it if you own DIGGER DOG.

TRUCK DOG
When she hears the jingle of the keys she's
ready to go any place, any time, with anybody.

Filching a Twinky out of a blind bag
while the boss snoozes is no challenge
at all for SNACK DOG.

GUARD DOG

He won't let anyone near your truck.
Not even your hunting buddies.

POOP DOG

No matter how fast
you scoop, he's always
one pile ahead of you.

DEAF DOG

He can hear a donut box open at 100 yards but he can't hear the whistle.

WATERFOWLING
HALL OF FAME

BENJAMIN FRANKLIN

Although primarily known as one of our founding fathers, Ben also invented the electric collar while flying a kite in a thunderstorm when the string became tangled around his neck.

BOYD "BACK ORDER" BABCOCK

Before Babcock invented the first catalog in 1932, duck hunters had to actually go into a store to purchase their gear.

JEREMIAH "JERKSTRING" JENKINS

Jeremiah carved the first battery powered duck decoy in 1889. The decoy sat on a shelf in his workshop for twenty years until the battery was invented.

On October 31, 1962
HARVEY "HIGHBALL" HARRINGTON
became the first duck hunter to set five alarm clocks the night before opening day, beating the previous record of four.

ORVILLE AND WILBUR ROBO

In September of 1990, after working unsuccessfully on a secret Defense Department contract to develop a new kind of helicopter, Orville and Wilbur reconfigured their prototype into the first spinning wing decoy.

FLOYD "FLYWAY" FLANNIGAN

In 1913 Floyd became the first married man to hunt
every day of the duck season for ten consecutive years.
His divorce was finalized in 1914.

In 1950
COTTONMOUTH COOPER

of Gumbo, Louisiana, became the first southern duck hunter to complain about northern waterfowl management areas short-stopping "OUR DUCKS."

Would you believe EVEN MORE words of WATERFOWLING WISDOM from Gadwall Gallagher?

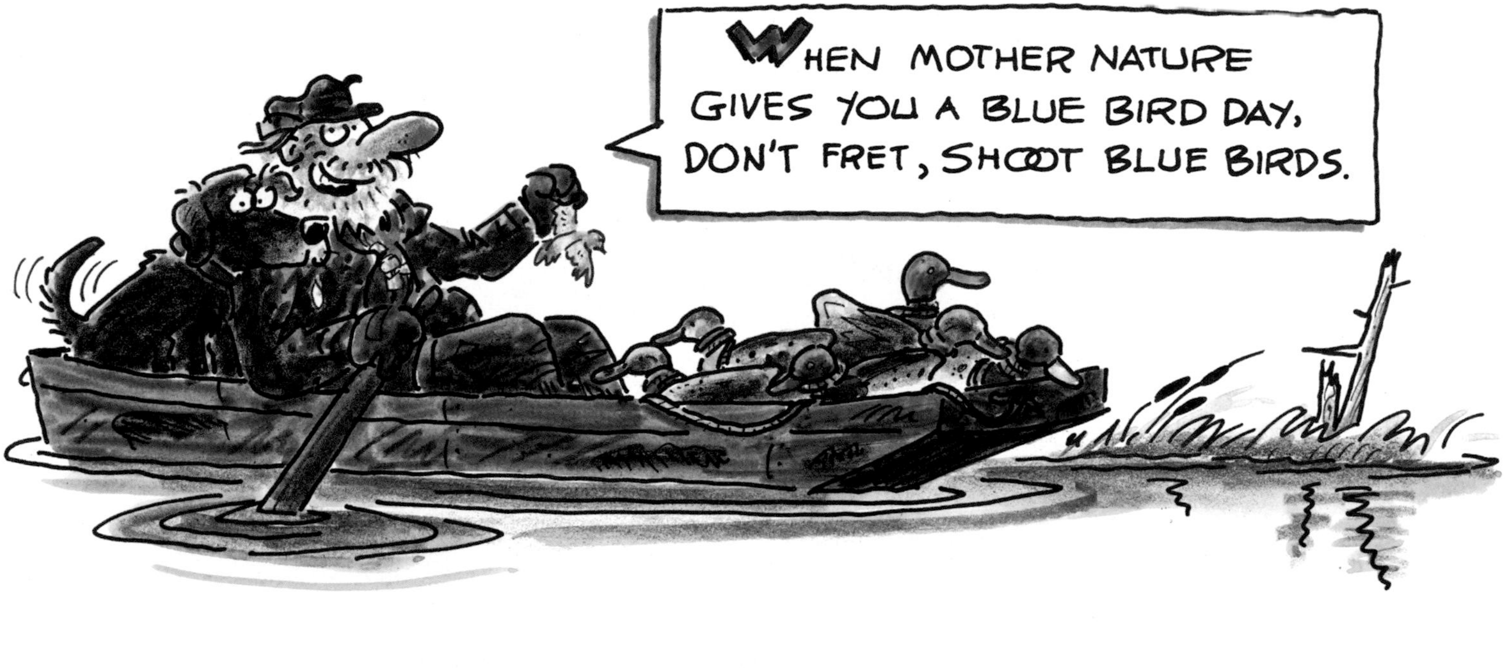
When mother nature gives you a blue bird day, don't fret, shoot blue birds.

THE FUTURE OF WATERFOWLING

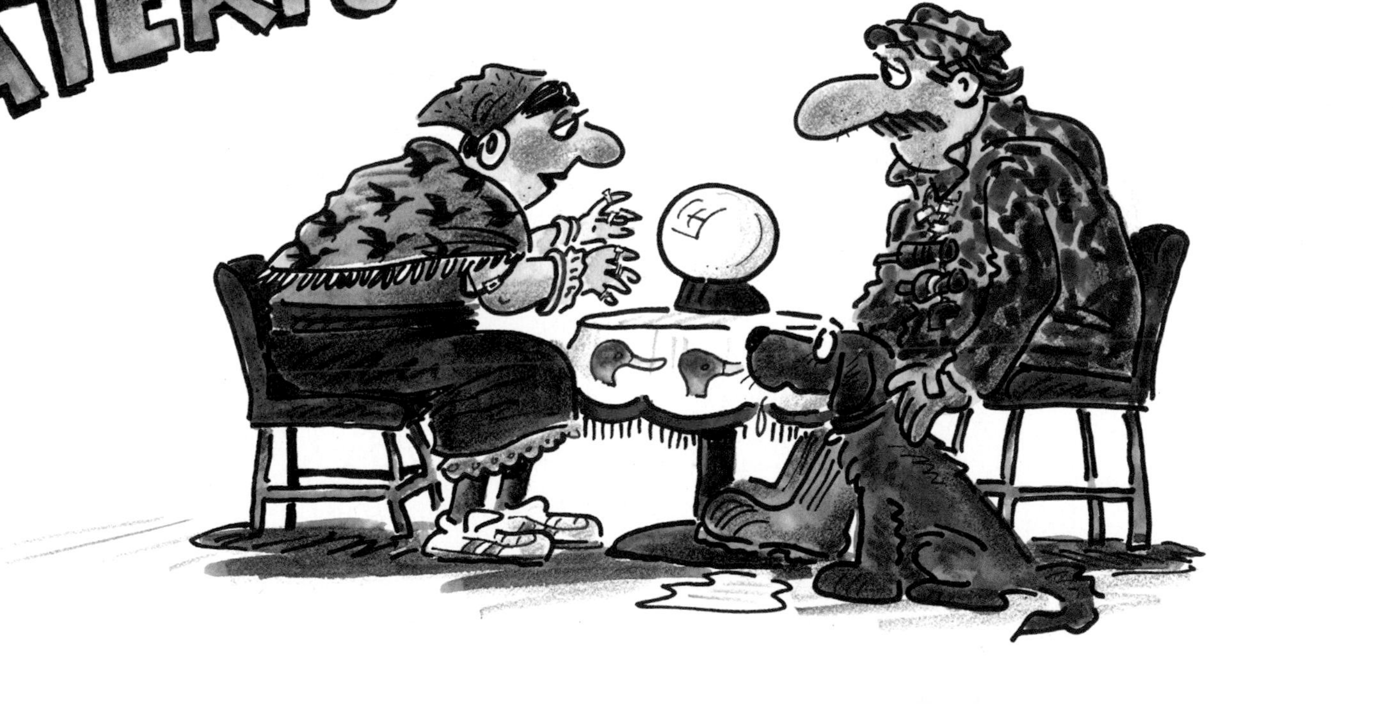

In an effort to stem the rising population of snow geese, hunters will be allowed to use hand grenades, bazookas, poison gas, and tactical nuclear weapons.

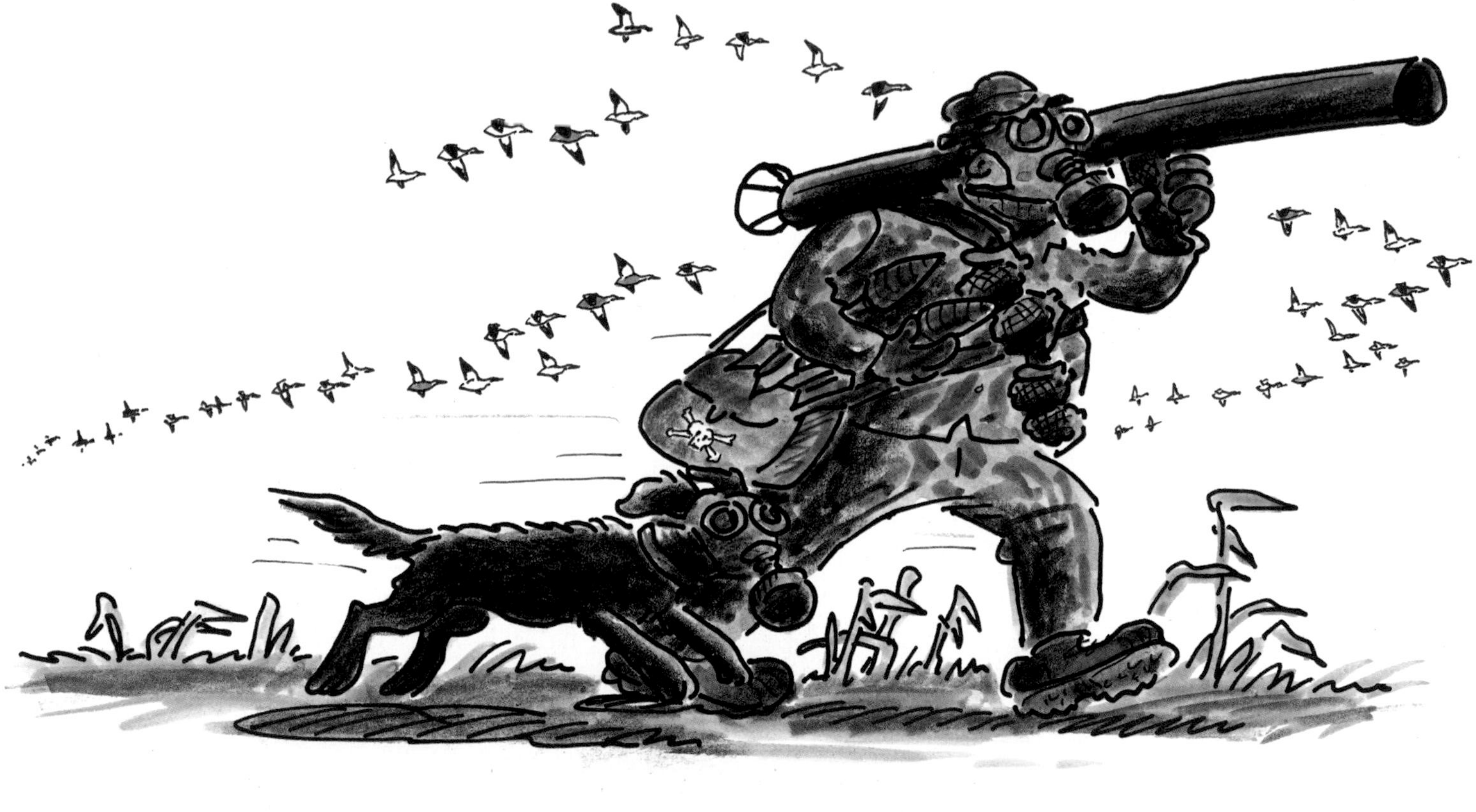

Taking a cue from their darker cousins, snow geese
will begin to congregate on golf courses, bringing
this silly game to an ignominious end.

The standard 12 gauge shotgun, chambered for 3-3.5 in. ammunition, will be replaced by the 5" Super-Duper Magnum. For safety reasons this weapon will be fired with the butt against the ground like a mortar.

Retrievers will be trained in the use of metal detectors to help them locate downed ducks full of steel shot.

Carrying the "pointing Lab" phenomenon to its logical conclusion, Labrador retrievers will be bred to put out decoys, build blinds, call ducks, and operate outboard motors.

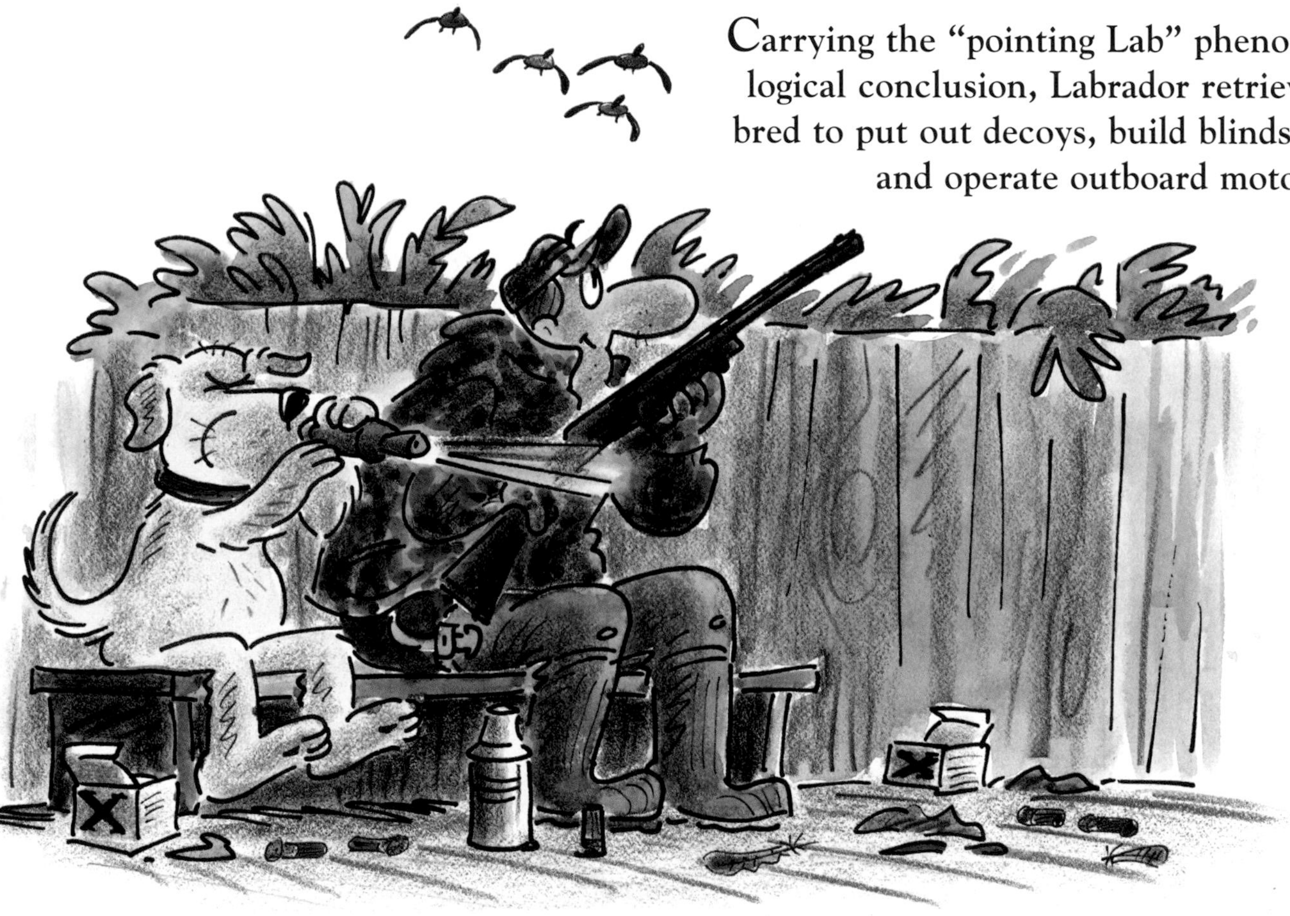

The average retriever, fed a steady diet of donuts,
Twinkies, HoHos, Ding Dongs, and Little Debbies,
will tip the scales at a sprightly 357 pounds.

And most amazing of all... somewhere, sometime, some lucky shot gunner will actually HIT a teal!

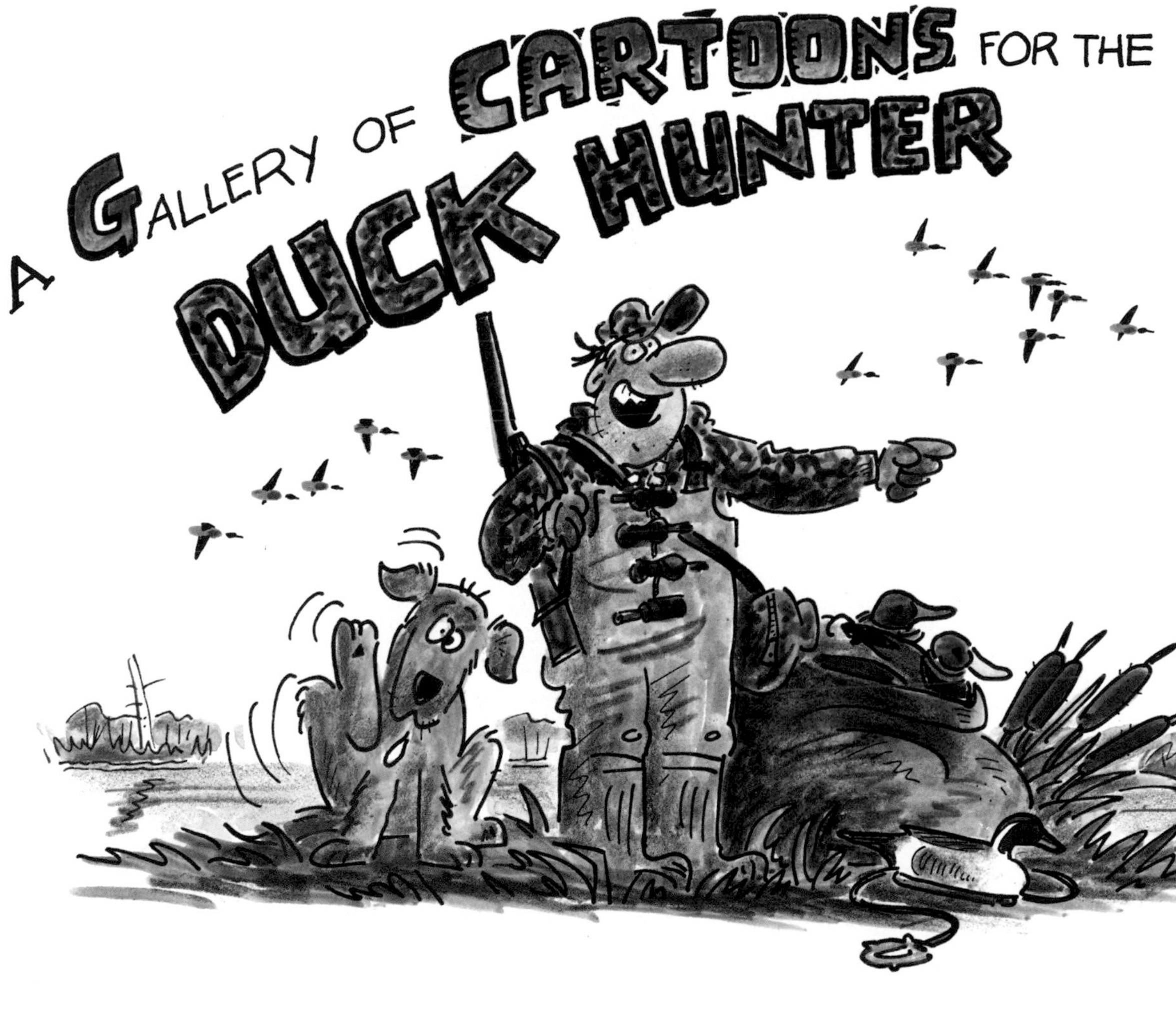
A GALLERY OF CARTOONS FOR THE DUCK HUNTER

"You men cut some brush for a blind while I put out the decoys."

COCHRAN!

"Tomorrow on Oprah, men who eat shovelers and the women who love them."

"I see the big redlegs have finally come down."

"Electric collar?! Dang! I thought it was a transistor radio."

FRED SOON REALIZED HE HAD A LOT TO LEARN ABOUT FLAGGING GEESE.

"Sometimes I wish I'd never taught him hand signals."

"Don't tip up to feed as long as he's behind you."

"It wasn't enough that you ate my cinnamon rolls…"

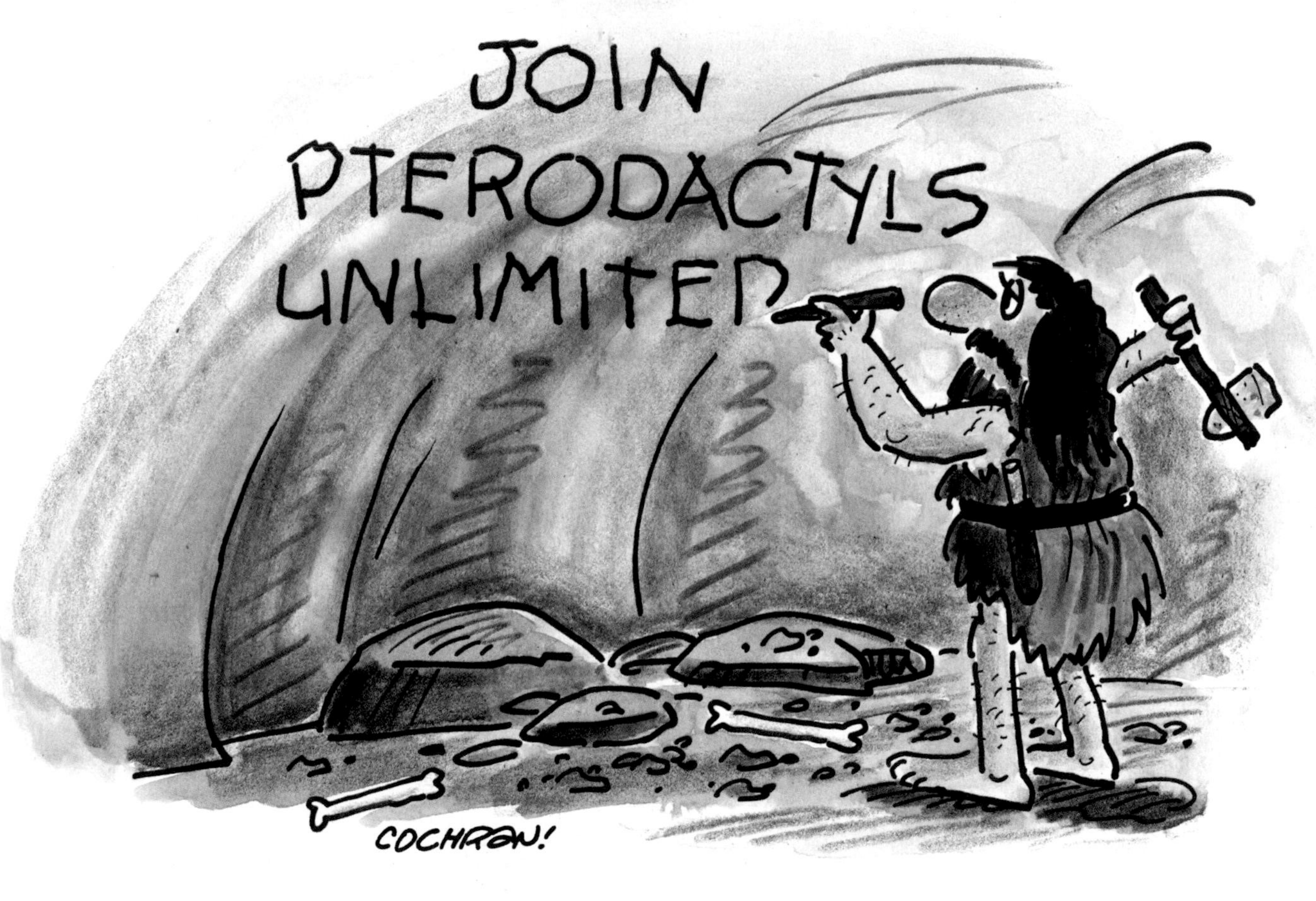
JOIN
PTERODACTYLS
UNLIMITED
COCHRAN!

"Build it and they will come."

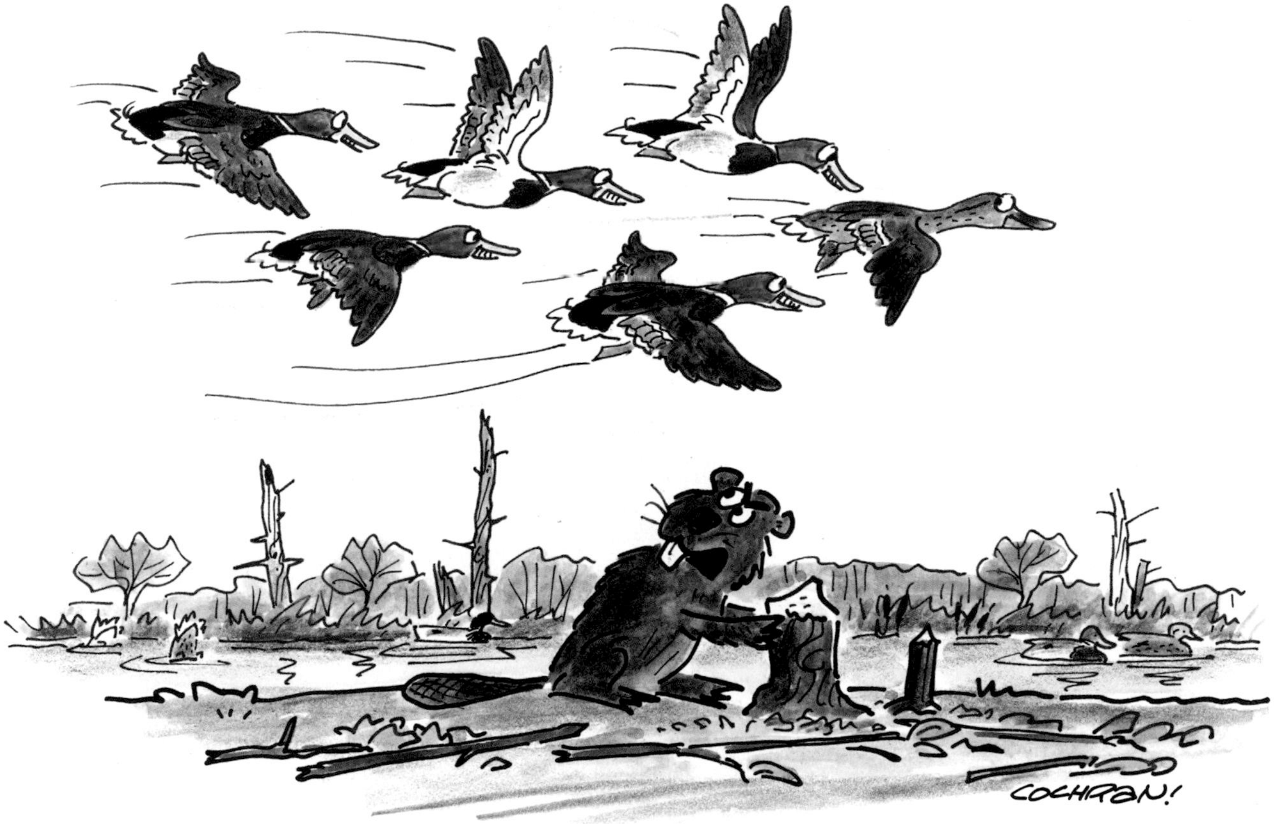
COCHRAN!

"Get a room!"

"Augusta… Pebble Beach… I've pooped on them all."

"Let's fly south. I mean, what can they do?... Shoot us?"

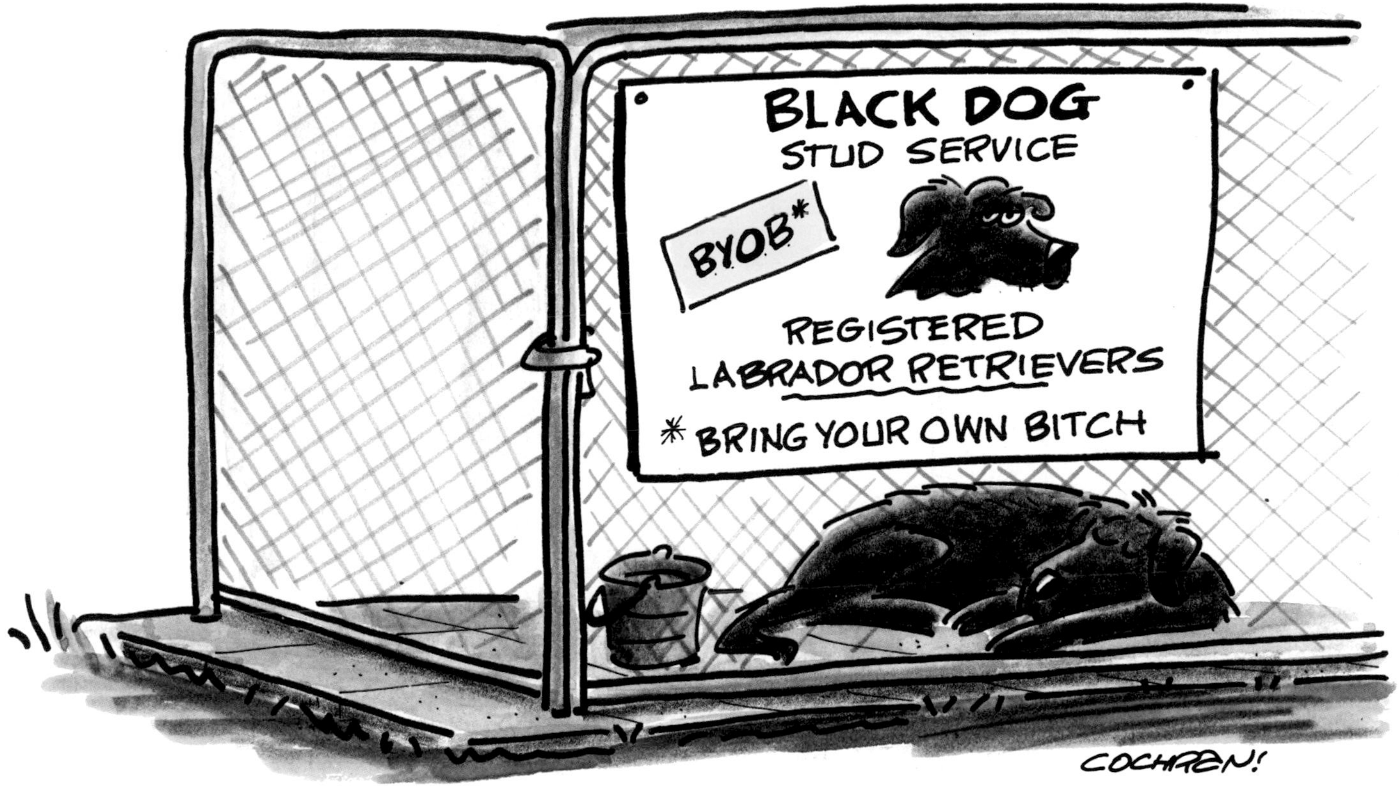
BLACK DOG
STUD SERVICE
BYOB*
REGISTERED
LABRADOR RETRIEVERS
* BRING YOUR OWN BITCH
COCHRAN!

The End